ANXIETY

ZERO

The constant search...

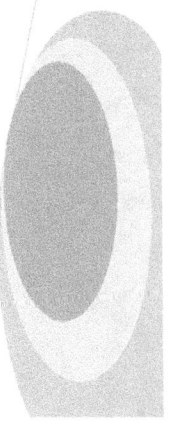

ANXIETY

ZERO

The constant search...

ANXIETY
ZERO

By Wladimir Moreira Dias

#

"If you are depressed you are living in the past. "

"If you are anxious you are living in the future."

"If you are at peace you are living in the present"

Thanks for cooperation and confidence of all.

ANXIETY ZERO

The constant search...

PREFACE

The term "anxiety" can be defined in several ways by the non-technical dictionaries: affliction, anguish, disturbance of the spirit caused by uncertainties in a context of danger, among others.

When the technical aspect is taken into account, we can understand anxiety as a phenomenon that can either benefit or damage us, depending on its circumstances or intensity, which may become pathological, i.e., anxiety may damage us both psychologically (mentally) and somatically (physically).

Anxiety stimulates the individual to act; however, when in excess, it does exactly the opposite, it stops people from reacting.

Frequently, depression brings a series of periodic harms, which can be very particular, especially in individuals with mood swings.

Such individuals go through strange emotional fluctuations, or mood swings. Sometimes, they see themselves on top of the world. They feel euphoric and exuberant, ready to do anything.

They can be serene and jubilant, but most of the time, such expansive mood radically changes to shyness and depression.

This book focus exactly on such individuals and proposes self-help techniques, teaching how to overcome such moments, through redirection and stimulation of thoughts.

17

TOPICS

-Presentation

-Depression

 -Anxiety-human relations

-Affliction

-Human Nature

-Analysis and comments

-Positivity

PRESENTATION

The anxiety disorders are diseases related to the functioning of the body and life experiences...

After some time, already in my room, I was looking at some photos of the island that were placed on the wall in front of my desk and also i was planning visit it, soon. Nevertheless, it still I was feeling a little depressed inside that room. Unfortunately, sometimes this happens to me, regardless of where I stayed or what I'm doing.

According to my friend Iohan, this kind of behavior is pretty common these days, mainly due to emotional stress to which we are all exposed continuously.

Maybe this sudden depression has been caused, paradoxically, by the emotional stability that was living on that farm, fairly rare thing in my life, always troubled and full of emotional bombing.

When this emotional instability happens to me, I search to meditate a little, in fact, like the monks hermits, discoverers of this island where I'm spending some few weeks on vacation and already were practiced since the year 700, searching for your inner balance.

I know that, generally speaking, the human brain faces a permanent conflict between its center of emotion, looking for immediate gratification, and the zone of reason, favoring the long-term goals.

Then I went to the balcony, where I liked to meditate, taking advantage also to contemplate the landscape of the farm, a bit atypical, and also to ponder a little about everything that was happening to me, with my emotions.

It reminded me of one of the movies that thrilled me: Bicentennial Man, with Robin Williams.

This film is an very original science fiction and tells the history of two centuries of quest for humanization undertaken by the main character.

However, those looking for this humanization are not a person, but rather a robot, a machine created by man to serve him.

This story, in fact, it is an interesting comedy, because it refers to a special machine, which left the factory with a "minor glitch".

This defect made her, at one moment; he to feel that could pursue an evolution beyond already defined by yours creators. The robot tried to be more human with yours passions and desires...
Sometimes I wonder if it is really possible to have a harmonic co-existence between logic and emotion into a single being, or if these conflicts will always exist, because our reality is a big maze of uncertainties.

I think we should keep our fears for ourselves and share our courage, but without hiding the fears in our underground castles. Let them trapped in cells through which we pass every day.

Listen, Yes, what they have to say, because that's what they do well. But leave them behind bars, serving a life sentence. And only drop your courage, controlling only so it doesn´t turn in arrogance.

I've always had the habit of reserving at least half an hour of the day for this kind of conceptual analysis that helps me to get a sense for life and cause me a good feeling, a sort of self-perception of values, which always helps me clarify my ideas and my conflicts.

I stood awhile out there, swinging on a Chair and thinking about a lot of things that are really almost integral part about our lives, like dreams, which unfortunately demonstrates that only dream our life is not to live it. Dreams can help us set goals, life goals, but on the other hand also frustrates us, disappoints and can change a lot things involving our emotional.

They include, on the one hand, the instinctive drives of nature and, on the other hand, include noble sentiments. I'm a fan of Jung's theory, that compares the human mind to a House, where the floors high, decorated with their personal objects, represent mental levels more aware and, as it descends, are universal elements, being that in your basement is our deepest unconscious.

I think the individual may achieve a great intellectual superiority and yet remain emotionally a baby. I think also that the emotional balance and maturity are essential ingredients for our self-development, but for this purpose we must acquire an intimate knowledge of ourselves, we must to set boundaries to our impulses, desires and dreams, seeking to achieve them in a way so rational and organized as possible.

One of the most valuable things we can learn about the cosmic laws is that everything has a heartbeat and follows a rhythm. Action and stagnation, emotion and reason, light and dark, time to sow and a time to harvest.

To live, breathe, have a heart and respiratory rate, with pauses and movements. This pulsation performs two important functions in order to recover a previous condition and prepare for another later.

Despite this involvement, almost never realized this pulse of energy, this harmony of life, which exists continuously, always defining movements, desires and values in our lives.

Then I decided to go back to my room.

It was when I found a local newspaper that was on the living room sofa. After reading some of their news a little more critically... so I could see very clearly that, regardless of where we are, it is always very difficult to make any analysis in the behavioral level, but really, there is no mistaking the face of harsh reality of lifetime.

Many live, but few live well. This is because the individual interests are almost always first, representing a very simple and human behavior, the need to stand out in the crowd.

The next morning, there I was again talking to Maryh. While finalizing the breakfast, we talked about cooking and she commented about a trip he had made to France; by the way, told me that nowhere else in the world the art of eating deserved as much attention as in this region.

- Herbs, cheeses and condiments combined gently with everything to provide unforgettable joy to palate caused for those sauces with sour cream base, also the unforgettable truffles, their wines, really have great memories of this country, she said.

I always curious, wanted to know if she already knew something about the Brazilian cuisine. She, half embarrassed, replied he did not know anything.

- Then you need to know it, Maryh because our cuisine is one of the richest in the world.

Do not miss the opportunity

- I said to her that always friendly continued talking as she sipped coffee.

At this moment, I admired through the kitchen window the beauties of a land where the fire and ice seemed in a battle.

When I heard Iohan calling me and inviting me to try some other liquors that had prepared, of course I accepted immediately because i loved those their liquors.

I always thought about Iohan like a very balanced person emotionally; perhaps their training in psychology has helped in this regard. Whenever we talked, I liked to explore a bit these knowledge related to the human psyche.

When I first came to the balcony I could see clearly that peace of mind that, for me, was her characteristic, moreover, its placidity impressed me greatly.

After experiencing one of its liqueurs, we started talking and I suddenly was just asking if in a place with such beautiful landscapes if he could get moody.

After my question, he looked at me and smiling, told me:

– Of course, but I've learned to control it very well, thanks to my course; and at the time we discussed a lot about this subject, incidentally, without exaggeration, I think I've exhausted, along with my colleagues, all its aspects.

And continued...

You know, usually when a person is led by a mood variable it turns out to feel those terrible depressions, which all of us at one time or another in our lives we witness, showing us that is, to some extent, completely normal.

However, throughout my life, I learned that as we mature, also learned, the search to improve my understanding consciously or unconsciously perhaps, about the real causes of these emotional fluctuations and step by step we become better prepared to overcome them and, believe me, this is a fight that lasts throughout our life.

After all, as we know, in just one day our mind can observe numerous situations and influence us positively or negatively on our mood and even when we do not realize, these social interference are always active and often for one reason or another, we don't manage well these huge amounts of emotional charge we receive, until ultimately define our state of mind, which becomes a simple product of the external environment to which we are exposed and often resulting in a bad mood.

I think this very interesting subject, on emotions

- I commented to Iohan, who readily agreed and continued...

For individuals better prepared, all and any antagonism is always seen as another challenge to be overcome.

The life forces flowing in them as a strong spring and elastic that cannot be suppressed forever and, in this way, we have matured.

On the other hand, there will be also easy periods in our lives.

When the winds blow in our favor, the outlook is bright, the joy of living is spontaneous and the will to achieve is unbreakable.

This can be that famous "our time", which happens a few times in our lives.

- Honestly told me and commented...

- I think the big secret to maintain emotional stability solely depends on the way we face the various panoramas of our lives and how we manage, i.e. the preparation of each makes a difference in the final result.

As they say what doesn't kill you surely make us stronger.

WHAT IS ANXIETY ZERO?

A constant search...

It will always be at the core of our emotions, being considered by many evil of the century.

The term "anxiety" can be defined in several ways by the non-technical dictionaries: affliction, anguish, disturbance of the spirit caused by uncertainties in a context of danger, among others.

When the technical aspect is taken into account, we can understand anxiety as a phenomenon that can either benefit or damage us, depending on its circumstances or intensity, which may become pathological, i.e., anxiety may damage us both psychologically (mentally) and somatically (physically).

Anxiety stimulates the individual to act; however, when in excess, it does exactly the opposite, it stops people from reacting.

CAUSES OF ANXIETY

Anxiety disorders are diseases related to the functioning of the body and life experiences.

The person may feel anxious most of the time no apparent reason or anxiety may have only sometimes, but so intensely feel immobilized.

The feeling of anxiety can be so uncomfortable that to avoid it, people stop doing simple things (like using the elevator) because of the discomfort they feel.

SYMPTOMS OF ANXIETY

The anxiety disorders are caused in a context with much more intense symptoms than that the normal anxiety of everyday life. They appear as:

Concerns, tensions or exaggerated fears (a person cannot relax).

Solid feel that a disaster or something very bad will happen

Exaggerated concerns about health, money, family or work

Extreme fear of an object or particular situation

Exaggerated fear of being publicly humiliated

Lack of control over thoughts, images or attitudes that are repeated regardless of what will happen always will exist a kind of feel with dread after a very difficult situation.

ANXIETY CONTROL

Medicines always with recipe and follow the medics.

Psychotherapy with psychologist or psychiatrist

Combination of both treatments (drugs and psychotherapy).

Most people with anxiety begins to feel better and resumes its activities after a few weeks of treatment.

So it is important to seek expert help at the health center nearest.

Early and accurate diagnosis of anxiety, effective treatment and follow-up for a long term are essential for better results and lower losses.

ANXIETY ZERO

The constant search...

When the individual is in a state of depressed mood, usually suffers greatly creating feelings of guilt and inferiority.

For him life has lost its charm, self-confidence shown extremely committed, until at last, begin to feed nihilistic desires.

His life seems a dark night that will never end, assuming often extreme proportions that without proper guidance can achieve even a degree often pathological.

However, when this individual has adequate counseling, which will bring undoubtedly, prevent these states distortion of ideas that create those terrible emotional instability, and that all of us at one time or another in our lives witnessed or felt to a greater or lesser degree, showing us that to some extent this is completely normal.

This is when our intellect becomes essential to achieve that heralded minimum inner balance and that allows us to enjoy a social life.

This balance will occur mostly in that we comprising consciously or unconsciously, the real causes of these emotional fluctuations, to which we are continually exposed, leaving us better prepared so that we can overcome them, because this is a never-ending struggle and lasts for a lifetime.

Our minds witness in one day, many situations that affect us positively or negatively on our mood, even when we do not realize, these social interference are always active.

In general, our mood is extremely susceptible to all kinds of external influence and often for one reason or another, do not manage these huge amounts of emotional charge we receive, until all these flows and external emotional ebbs ultimately define the our mood, creating an unconscious psychic atmosphere in which we are no longer masters of our more humor, it becomes a simple product of the external environment in which we are exposed, often resulting in a bad mood.

However, there are also easy periods in our lives when all the winds blow in our favor, the outlook is bright, the joy of living is spontaneous and the will to achieve is unbreakable.

This can be that famous "our time" that happens a few times in our lives, and therefore, it is prudent to take maximum advantage of it, but always taking due care not to become overconfident and end creating an opinion of himself, far short of their reality, which certainly will bring strong future frustrations.

Often when a person gets involved by the enthusiastic excitement that apparent success, which often leads to excess, mistreating others and antagonizing many interests, causing what is called social reflux, i.e. a strong reaction of the people the fence, creating a never-ending atmosphere of dismay on his back, eventually even more obscure your mental horizon, contributing to an imminent worsening of possible depression.

However, for the best prepared individuals, any antagonism is always seen as another challenge to be overcome.

The life force flows in them as a strong and elastic spring which cannot be suppressed forever and with it matures and grows stronger. In general terms, our emotional mood largely determines our way of thinking.

At a time of deep sorrow can only perceive sad facts and so does most joyful times, when only perceive facts that lead us to a euphoric mood.

It is desirable to always act with care during these phases of rise of the emotional mood.

The big secret to keep away from depression is based on how we view the various landscapes that form in the course of our lives and how we manage, that is, the preparation of each makes a difference in the final result of this endless struggle against depression, meaning more or less balance emotional balance.

It is always important to keep in mind, especially in those moments of utter despair that you cannot intellectualize absolutely nothing, that everything passes and nothing is really so fundamental that can supplant importance in the lifetime opportunity.

Meditation is undoubtedly one of the most efficient techniques when seeking inner balance and regular practice can become a powerful weapon against depression.

To the extent that the individual is improved this technique, he begins to consider depression as a mere transitory mental state, facilitating much their friendship with her.

Efficiently used by those who meditate, when they tend to fall into a deep depression, is to seek in meditation, the strength they need to prevent the spread of it within themselves, using mainly a thorough analysis, a type of self perception of values, for the clarification of ideas, because in this context knowing the causes of depression, you can dispel it very easily and shift its focus all your mental energy.

It contributes to the individual to find and can better understand their origins, making it more stable and less susceptible to external changes that are reflected in the customs and social trends around you and it could unbalance him many times.

This decrease occurs influences the extent that it will realize that each stage of life has the meaning or importance when moving towards maturity. It appears as the basis of all our psychological problems.

Ultimately, all our mental, neurotic and psychotic disorders have their origin in anxiety, and other physical ailments, such as insomnia, headache, heart problems and pressure.

Anxiety is not restricted to any particular stage of life or any group of people, their characteristics penetrates all human situations, and acts directly at the heart of our emotions.

She is not related to any specific object or attitude and almost always expressed as an unintelligible evil, meaning a mental restlessness, which seems to have no objectivity.

Any more specific approach to the problem of anxiety, requires prior knowledge of the different ways in which it acts in our mind, that is, there are two ways the expression of anxiety within the mind, direct and indirect.

The direct causes psychic repression and indirect manifests as a result of this repression, resulting in a growing inner tension reflected in the mind without the mind has any definite knowledge of what is happening.

Anyway, anxiety is an inevitable accompaniment of life within the development process and it is up to us through the art of living, the improvement of the techniques and skills needed for better integration between her and this ongoing renaissance that is life.

The wisdom in human relations is the mark of a mature personality that leads to happiness in life and also to spiritual development.

It is essential for our inner growth and well-being.

Our life is made up of various plans, requiring a relative balance between them to have a productive and happy life.

For example, for an individual to build a successful career, not just only the know-how or the equipment they have, but weighs a lot for this success the quality of people he knows, that is, this one's future success certainly not will simply be a product of how much skill he had, but mostly how he managed to harmonize with those people who at one time or another of his professional life, participated in contributing or delaying this your way.

When developing the skill in dealing with people within their interaction, the possibility of emotional fluctuations decreases a lot.

However when you do not have this skill, your problems are sure to multiply, leading you to alienation and social antagonism, the pressure will be much greater, damaging that your minimum balance, so necessary for their constructive development and spiritual fulfillment.

This is because the fundamental goal of human life is essentially linked to the concept of human relationships and the more she realizes this essence, the clearer becomes your cosmic vision of prosperity, resulting in a social life more significant and fruitful.

Depression along with the hurt and the like are afflictions of the mind and may disappear without reaching the level of despair, but this goes much deeper, affects the very core of human existence.

It is an emotional disorder, a disease of the mind, more or less transient, despair is much more chronic is a disease of the soul. All these states cause suffering, universally experienced, creating a natural impulse of all living creatures in the sense always avoid it.

When we think of pain, always comes a somewhat derogatory connotation, a negative fact.

However, when we think of pleasure everything changes, because it is the goal of all axial forces, being an essential ingredient to the state of happiness and that humans suffer more intensely when it becomes aware of his own limitations. However, his deepest suffering, in a paradox, is also its moment of greatest joy.

In the very act of clearly recognize its limitations, in a sense, it transcends all limitations and sees unlimited dwelling deep inside your being, surrounded by numerous limitations.

So pain and pleasure come together in this exalted moment of enlightenment, defining as the supreme goal of life, a dynamic happiness that integrates itself, pain and pleasure.

Moderation: when passion and reason, nature and the spirit must be led by a dynamic harmony.

Without the guidance of reason, passion of life is lost in autodissipação, in the chaos of conflicting impulses, which are reflected in the spirit.

Body discipline: when the body has to be prepared, as a tool to search for a deeper spiritual life.

Concentration: that is an essential step in meditation and is to mobilize the resources of the mind in one direction, focusing on the mental energy on a defined target.

Self-observation: it is the time of abandonment, of complete relaxation. We left the body and the mind in freedom and decided to do nothing.

Discernment: consisting in concentration and self impartial observation, seeking relief from the stresses and strains of daily life, involving relaxation and self emptying.

Lighting: without it, meditation is reduced to a futile exercise, because it is the soul of meditation, is the perception of being.

Dedication: is the final stage of meditation and consists of an active dedication to cosmic prosperity, representing the time in which the perception of your being is integrated with the universe.

Some hiking trails, is the sensitivity that dominates, it is what governs their goals, very damaging your emotional stability, preventing more objective judgments of facts, finally a slave sensitivity.

They fill their lives with dreams, daydreams, but dream life, not live it.

You need to move on, if you use it yes, it is good to dream, but just as motivating actions.

Dreams help us to trace goals, life goals, but on the other hand also frustrates us, disappoint us and moves a lot with our emotional, which is the most vital aspect of human personality.

It covers on the one hand, the instinctive impulses of nature and the other includes noble sentiments.

The individual can achieve a great intellectual superiority and yet remain emotionally a baby.

The emotional balance and maturity are essential ingredients for self development, but for this purpose, we have to acquire an intimate knowledge of ourselves, we have to set limits to our impulses, desires and dreams, seeking to carry them out in such a rational way and organized as possible.

Since childhood the fact of death is a fact that attracts our attention, whether we like it or not. We cannot live indifferent to it, because our whole life structure is based on this phenomenon.

However, most people seek to move away from this subject, so terribly disturbing, creating an immense emotional and unresolved that torments the individual throughout his life, paralyzing its initiative and suffocating his spirit, causing intense emotional fluctuations.

Death in mind operates like a black question mark and how the individual addresses this question in his mind, determines all your way of life and therefore is an issue that has to be solved first of all, each should research, exchange ideas and find your truth to this as natural and intriguing phenomenon of life.

It is the harmony. When the whole existence becomes unified in which all apparent contradictions are reconciled.

There can be no happiness without adequate self-development, as there are many conflicting tendencies in our nature. A painful mistake is to take this or that desire too far, never give utmost importance to this or that aspect of life at the expense of everyone else.

Should be first of all a self intelligent organization within our lives, which is the fundamental principle to achieve a balanced life.

We always have a multitude of desires, apparently conflicting and intertwined in our mind, there are different primitive impulses, rational, selfish, altruistic and all give always be administered as goal seeking the spirit of intelligent cooperation between nature and spirit, for without spirit nature is blind and without nature spirit is crippled, finally in life, happiness can be achieved only when it follows the law of proper distribution, which is the operating principle of harmony concept.

In this great adventure that is life, we expect a miracle every day, but we forget that this miracle this within ourselves, life itself.

We live in a bath of sensations, of which a small part attracts our attention and that we seek in religion, art and science, the great meaning of life, but experience teaches us that not all roads are for all walkers.

This is because some forget to help your inner dawn to sunrise and end up living a dull existence that does not mean success or money, but simply a balanced and well-lived life.

Our reality is often less dramatic than the view we have of it, we should always be an optimist vigilant, renewing our energy all the time, purifying our thoughts with a healthy imagination, trying to keep the mind always vigorous and quiet, after all into the skin, all the problems are psychological.

For the optimist, what matters is knowing that now, at this very moment, are being born, growing rich and pure opportunities, that the noblest essence of life makes flow in millions of beings, in all parts of the world, because who of us has the privilege of losing the flow, the vibrant abstractions of life which only manifest themselves through positivism, so always be positive, upbeat, optimistic, cheerful, that emotional fluctuations are increasingly distant from his heart and his life.

ANALYSIS AND COMMENTS

Do you suffer with anticipation? Wake up tired? Does not tolerate working with slow people?

Have headaches or muscle?

You forget things easily? If you answered" 'yes" to any of these questions, it is likely to suffer the Accelerated Thinking Syndrome (SPA).

Considered by the psychiatrists as the new evil of the century, overcoming depression, it affects much of the world population.

In this book, you will understand how the human mind to be able to slow down your thoughts, manage your emotion effectively and redeem their quality of life.

Here contains some latest information on the progress of science in the treatment of emotional disorders.

Written clearly and simply, your goal is to rethink the paradigm body / mind, object reflections from Plato.

In this book we seek the foundations of medicine of Emotions, prescribing some methods to heal: integration neuro emotional by eye movements, heart rate regulation, synchronization of the biological clock, acupuncture, exercise, intake of the substance Omega 3 and communication techniques affective.

Although there are no sure-fire recipes for good health, we search the full health without prescription term, rs.

Our social order and the environment in which we live have changed in the last fifty years.

And the chances of the pace of these changes increase and, consequently, more and more people suffer from anxiety disorder are gigantic.

Certain techniques can show us that even before all the chaos of our routine, we can live more peacefully and more with peaceful.

There are simple and natural tools that will help you get rid of this evil that both affect their quality of life.

This way, you will feel much more confident calm and safe to meet the daily challenges.

Do not wait, because or you end up with the Anxiety Before or it ends with you!

You can stop being anxious?

No, definitely not, because we need the anxiety mechanism to survive. So you must be wondering: how does a person to be less anxious to get rid of the torments of the negative anxiety? Anxiety means not being in here and right now.

So if what more do inside our head is thinking about a number of things at the same time, it is almost certain that we are never in the present moment, generating a negative anxiety and most psychosomatic symptoms caused by it.

Anxiety disorders are the most common psychiatric illness and result in functional impairment and considerable suffering.

Based on recent developments in research on the mechanisms of these disorders and the response to treatment, concise and easy to understand texts, cover the following topics: epidemiology and co morbidity, diagnosis and differential diagnosis, biological theories and psychological and treatment by medication, psychotherapy or combined approaches.

The main anxiety disorders presented in this book are: panic disorder, generalized anxiety disorder, social phobia, specific phobias, obsessive-compulsive disorder and post-traumatic stress disorder.

It is the traffic? The car payment?

The novel that does not go well?

The pressure of the boss?

The feeling of never achieve what you want?

Anxiety may be undermining your life.

And with that, disrupting their daily lives and their future.

Learn to control this plague of modern times seek simple tips that will help you turn your life into something worth enjoying.

In our contemporary life, becomes indispensable, to investigate the origins of anxiety and teaches how to live a less stressful life.

Using the methods and techniques proposed, based on the best psychological treatments available, we can win a seizure-free life, tension and excitement related to anxiety.

All people go through some kind of concern about the major decisions of life wedding day jitters to anxiety in a new job.

But what about the more 'quiet' fears, less noticeable, which relate to everyday choices and relationships with others?

The intimate fears, change or errors may seem cliché, but for most people, most common anxieties as these can act as unwitting saboteurs.

And are there some recent research in psychology and neuroscience to reaffirm that the biggest barrier to happiness is fear.

Brain imaging studies show that when fear is viewed from other angles, the individual is less likely to suffer from it.

But what about the more 'quiet' fears, less noticeable, which relate to everyday choices and relationships with others?

The intimate fears, change or errors may seem cliché, but for most people, most common anxieties as these can act as saboteurs unwitting.

Inspired by the meditative practices of the East, mindfulness is a powerful self-help tool that teaches us to live consciously in the present moment, dominate the negative thoughts and fail to react to everything on autopilot.

Seek a more comprehensive analysis of inner you and your emotions, find time meddling in simple techniques and are immensely effective, helping us to live a way more peaceful, intelligent and positive.

The most common forms of ODA (anxiety, panic and depression), allowing readers to learn the difference between individual and social fears, between panic and generalized anxiety disorder, and more.

Some people become experts by empirical living situation because end up accumulating decades of personal experience in the trenches against ODA, having experienced the problem since adolescence.

Let's work an atmosphere of confidentiality and reliability, as well as the scientific approach that make the theme a natural achievement.

Raise your hand if you have never suffered due to insecurity or told himself " I do not know dealing with relationships " .

Someone Else? Or ever lost sleep because of a fight, or to have the impression that things were over for the morning did realize that a storm in a glass of water?

It's not easy to be waiting for the response from the other.

It is less easy still be looking for signs confirming that the two not only want the same thing as share the same desire to be together forever.

Many people suffer from a sense of fragility and almost eternal sure that your relationships will not work, either because they think they will be left or because they believe they will never be loved at the same intensity of his feeling.

If you are ready to stop repeating the same mistakes, here are some techniques that can show you how to get the love it deserves and, even better, how to keep it.

Divided into four parts, you'll discover how their conflicts arose, initiate change dealing with the obstacles that keep you from cultivating happy relationships, create intimate relationships feeling safer and find someone who can make plan. Yes, that's the best part!

It is time to stop the suffering and torture of spending hours on end wondering if you are still well or are about to go through a crisis. Take the time insecurity of life and discover the love light.

The second issue of Anxiety Disorders aims to offer the reader up to date, objective and structured information about the different forms of anxiety and clinical presentations of anxiety disorders, believing this will have repercussions in mitigating the suffering of patients, often misunderstood, even by family members.

]

It is learned widespread doctor that the more accurate the diagnosis, the most appropriate therapeutic treatment and the greater the chances of recovery.

Anxiety disorders are common and limiting, undermining the social, family, academic and professional performance, but have (all without exception) effective treatment, and your goals remission, sustained remission and recovery. This book is primarily directed to psychiatrists, but may be of interest to colleagues in other specialties, those who work with family health and mental health professionals in general.

This is because, surely, all anxious and examine patients with anxiety disorders in their daily practice, probably more often than you think.

Diseases such as depression, generalized anxiety, panic disorder, OCD, alcohol abuse and illegal drugs, bipolar disorder, schizophrenia and Alzheimer's disease affect one in three people over a lifetime. To provide information about these disorders poorly diagnosed and treated, removing the mistaken notion that the diseases of the mind are nothing but weakness, freshness, character flaw or "invention people's heads ", the authors present here an accessible guide to all those interested in the subject.

After reports of individuals who have overcome or are recovering from an emotional disorder, the work helps to identify the line between normal human vagaries of psychic disorders.

And, with the support of experts in the mental health area, explains m up some of the origins d emotional disorders, the symptoms by which they manifest the treatments available on the NHS and in private services, prospects of cure and control, tips on how the family can help to circumvent the problem and what to do to prevent such diseases.

What cannot is settling. Fight and always seek support family and friends.

There are methods to combat anxiety based on the principles of cognitive-behavioral therapy (CBT).

In these cases, use of therapies and patient sessions will learn to understand and to better work their anxiety, identifying and challenging automatic thoughts.

Will practice how to face their fears in a safe and structured manner, through supervised exposure and homework assignments.

Obviously children are not free from this evil.

All children experience concerns.

Help them understand what is a concern, where she comes from and how to face it, is the first step to overcome anxieties.

Try to help them or teach them to stop and think twice, trying to see their concerns as they are.

Showing new ways to evaluate and overcome the fear of psychological point of view, physical and spiritual, creatively, which certainly will help your child to find the confidence and the courage to say: no more Worries!

Raise your hand if you have never suffered due to insecurity or told himself " I do not know dealing with relationships " .

Or so never lost sleep over a kind of fight, or to have the impression that thing the next morning... you simply realize you made a storm in a glass of water?

It's not easy to be waiting for an answer on the other.

It's less easy still be seeking signs that confirm that the two not only want the same thing as they share the same desire to be together forever.

Many people suffer from a sense of fragility and almost eternal sure that your relationships will not certain, either because they think will be left or because they believe they will never be loved at the same intensity of his feeling.

It is time to stop the suffering and torture of spending hours on end wondering if you are still well or are about to go through a crisis.

Take the time insecurity of life and discover the love light.

POSITIVE MENTAL IMAGES

Always start your day with: "Have a day full of happiness" and make it work in your favor.

The ultimate goal of life is harmony.

When the whole existence becomes unified in which all apparent contradictions are reconciled.

There can be no happiness without an appropriate self development, because there are many conflicting trends in our nature.

A painful mistake, is to take this or that desire too far, you should never give the utmost importance to this or that aspect of life, at the expense of everyone else.

It should be SEARCH be first of all a self - intelligent organization within our lives, which is the fundamental principle to really get a really balanced, happy life and sociable.

We always have a multitude of desires, apparently conflicting and intertwined in our mind, there are different primitive impulses, rational, selfish, altruistic, among others, and all should be well administered always seeking as a primary goal the spirit of intelligent cooperation between nature and the spirit, because without the spirit nature is blind and without nature spirit is crippled, finally in life, happiness can be achieved only when it follows the law of proper distribution, which is the principle of harmony op-proliferative concept.

When we look between the lines of this great adventure that is life, hope every day some kind of miracle, but we forget that this miracle this within ourselves, life itself.

We live in a bath of sensations, of which a small part attracts our attention and that we seek in religion, art and science, the great meaning of life, but experience teaches us that not all roads are for all walkers.

This is because some forget to help your inner dawn to sunrise and end up living a dull existence that does not mean success or money, but simply a balanced and well-lived life.

Our reality is often less dramatic than the view we have of it, we should always be an optimist vigilant, renewing our energy all the time, purifying our thoughts with a healthy imagination, trying to keep the mind always vigorous and quiet, after all the skin into all the problems are psychological, what matters is that now at this very moment, are being born, growing rich and pure opportunities which the noblest essence of life is flowing in millions of people in all parts of the world because who among us has the privilege of losing flowing, vibrant abstraction of life, which only manifest themselves through positivism, so always be positive, upbeat, optimistic, cheerful, emotional fluctuations that are increasingly distant from their heart and your life. Start your day always visualizing:

"I will have a full day of happiness" and
make reality work in your favor."

"The problem of individuals eager will always
be thoughts in excess, rs."

"When I despair, I remember that all through history the way of truth and love has always won. There have been tyrants and murderers and for a time they seem invincible, but in the end, they always fall – think of it, always."

Mahatma Gandhi

"Change your thoughts and you change your world!!!"

INFORMATION AND PUBLICATIONS

Twitter: AUTOR_WLADIMIR

INTERNATIONAL SITES

- Argentina
- Australia
- Austria
- Belgium
- Canada
- Czech Republic
- Denmark
- Finland
- France
- Germany
- Greece
- Hong Kong
- Hungary
- India
- Ireland
- Israel
- Italy
- Japan
- Korea
- Mexico
- Netherlands
- New Zealand
- Norway
- Portugal
- Romania
- Russian Federation
- Singapore
- Slovak Republic
- Spain
- Sweden
- Switzerland
- Taiwan
- Turkey

Blogger: authorwladimirdias.blogspot.com

About the Author: Wladimir Moreira Dias was born in Sao Paulo, state of Sao Paulo. He writes chronicles, having achieved second place in the Seventh International Literature Contest. He is the author of several successful books, currently sold in more than 15,000 bookstores around the world. He has a bachelor degree in Electric Engineering by FACENS/SP, with post-graduation in Production Engineering. He had an outstanding participation in the Literature Award of Sao Paulo, 2011, and in the Fifth Award for Authors in Contemporary Literature, 2014. He has more than 30 books published in several languages. He is also an expert in Language and Sociology due to his studies in Cambridge, United Kingdom. At present, he lives and works in "Baixada Santista", city of Santos, state of Sao Paulo.